GOOD DOGS

Scripture and Bible Verses from Your Best Friend

Becca Anderson

Coral gables

Published by Mango Publishing Group, a division of Mango Media Inc.

Cover Design: Morgane Leoni
Interior Layout: Roberto Nuñez
Photos Credits: Shutterstock

For permission requests, please contact the publisher at:
Mango Publishing Group
2850 S Douglas Road, 2nd Floor
Coral Gables, FL 33134 USA
info@mango.bz

For special orders, quantity sales, course adoptions and corporate sales, please email the publisher at sales@mango.bz. For trade and wholesale sales, please contact Ingram Publisher Services at: customer.service@ingramcontent.com or +1.800.509.4887.

Good Dogs: Scripture and Bible Verses from Your Best Friend

Library of Congress Cataloging-in-Publication number: 2020933911
ISBN: (print) 978-1-64250-248-0, (ebook)978-1-64250-249-7
BISAC category code REL012040, RELIGION / Christian Living / Inspirational

Printed in the United States of America

"I think God will have prepared everything for our perfect happiness. If it takes my dog being there in Heaven, I believe he'll be there."

Rev. Billy Graham

TABLE OF CONTENTS

Foreword

Everyone I know who has a dog is one step closer to heaven. First of all, dogs are simply the best at unconditional love. When you have the companionship of a canine, you experience love at the highest level. My friend Nancy has suffered a lot of loss in her life and was abandoned on a doorstep as a child. When you suffer the most primal of rejections (in her case, from both parents) without ever knowing why, you will have the kind of emotional wound that can almost never be healed. She always had lots of cool cats as pets but, until she got her Jack Russell terrier, Lizzy, she never knew truly unconditional love.

Turns out, Lizzy had also been abandoned and was at a shelter and deemed unadoptable: she was an older dog and no one wanted the aging canine, despite her winsome gaze. A neighbor told Nancy about Lizzy and she went over and fell in love. The feeling is very much mutual, and they are a sweet pair that just exudes love everywhere they go.

I was lucky to have grown up with dogs on the family farm. I have never known life without dogs and I think no one should! My Uncle Wilbur was a beloved preacher and one of his maxims was that "dogliness is next to godliness." He said that dogs protect their flock, even if it is just one person. He also thought that dogs like to be in a group to help keep each other fed and safe and that a dog's ability to express love is a direct gift from God.

If you know a lonely person or someone who needs a big dose of love in their life, suggest that they get a dog. It will absolutely change their life in the best possible way.

Let Dog be your copilot!

XOXO BECCA

FAITH

The Lord is the one who is shepherding me;
I lack nothing. He causes me to lie down in
pastures of green grass; he guides me beside
quiet waters. He revives my life; he leads me
in pathways that are righteous for the sake of
his name. Even when I walk through the valley
of the shadow of death, I will not be afraid
because you are with me. Your rod and your
staff—they comfort me.

PSALM 23:1-4

Like wandering sheep, we are prone to lose our way when faced with difficult choices. God is always there to guide us back and nurture our souls.

"For I know the plans that I have for you,' declares the Lord, 'plans for well-being, and not for calamity, in order to give you a future and a hope."

JEREMIAH 29:11

Everyone has the ability to live a virtuous and fulfilling life. The choice to do evil rather than good is not God's plan, but human fault.

"Look! God—yes God—is my salvation; I will trust, and not be afraid. For the Lord is my strength and my song, and he has become my salvation."

ISAIAH 12:2

Fear can take hold of your mind and keep you from being open to loving others and experiencing life fully. Embrace the unknown, the Lord will look out for you.

For I am convinced that neither death, nor life, nor angels, nor rulers, nor things present, nor things to come, nor powers, nor anything above, nor anything below, nor anything else in all creation can separate us from the love of God that is ours in union with the Messiah Jesus, our Lord.

ROMANS 8:38-39

God is there in good times and times of despair and oppression. There are no barriers to His love and guidance—He is always with you.

The Lord is my strength and my shield; my heart trusted in him, and I received help. My heart rejoices, and I give thanks to him with my song. The Lord is the strength of his people; he is a refuge of deliverance for his anointed.

PSALM 28:7-8

Wake each morning knowing that you have the strength of God backing you every day. No matter what struggle you face, you are not alone.

And we know that for those who love God, that is, for those who are called according to his purpose, all things are working together for good.

ROMANS 8:28

Opportunities will rise in your life that will give you the chance to make a difference. Take them. Doing good creates more good.

Trust in the Lord with all your heart, and do not depend on your own understanding. In all your ways acknowledge him, and He will make your paths straight.

PROVERBS 3:5-6

Thinking before acting is a basic step before making any decision. Prayer is the best way to reflect and include God in your plans.

Now faith is the assurance that what we hope for will come about and the certainty that what we cannot see exists.

HEBREWS 11:1

It often feels hard to trust the world around us when deception is so prevalent. Trust those who have the determination to love and do good, even if they may fail.

No temptation has overtaken you that is unusual for human beings. But God is faithful, and He will not allow you to be tempted beyond your strength. Instead, along with the temptation He will also provide a way out, so that you may be able to endure it.

1 CORINTHIANS 10:13

Everyone has struggled with the desire to make the wrong choice. Nothing is beyond your strength to resist if you allow God to guide you.

I've commanded you, haven't I? Be strong and courageous. Don't be fearful or discouraged, because the Lord your God is with you wherever you go.

JOSHUA 1:9

Your first reaction to an unpleasant situation may be fear, or anger, or melancholy. Aim to view all things with hope and remember the hand of God is there.

Never worry about anything. Instead, in every situation let your petitions be made known to God through prayers and requests, with thanksgiving.

PHILIPPIANS 4:6

There are many things you can't control in life. Give them to God and you will be relieved.

If you declare with your mouth that Jesus is Lord, and believe in your heart that God raised him from the dead, you will be saved. For one believes with his heart and is justified, and declares with his mouth and is saved.

ROMANS 10:9-10

Your convictions are among the most important elements of your character. Believe in good things, be thoughtful about them, and share that wisdom with others.

Cast on the Lord whatever he sends your way, and he will sustain you. He will never allow the righteous to be shaken.

PSALM 55:22

Though it may seem that evil often succeeds. With perseverance, goodness will triumph. The unjust will have their due, though it may take time.

The Spirit and the bride say, "Come!"
Let everyone who hears this say, "Come!"
Let everyone who is thirsty come!
Let anyone who wants the water of life take it as a gift!

REVELATION 22:17

Christ sacrificed himself for all humanity. Anyone who has sinned can be saved if they desire His love, everyone is deserving of it.

The Lord is my strength and protector, for he has become my deliverer. There's exultation for deliverance in the tents of the righteous: "The right hand of the Lord is victorious! The right hand of the Lord is exalted! The right hand of the Lord is victorious!"

PSALM 118:14-16

Take joy in the fact that God is with you. Let it give you hope and mettle when it seems that you have nothing to guide you.

You are my fortress and shield; I hope in your word. Leave me, you who practice evil, that I may observe the commands of my God.

PSALM 119:114-115

Take shelter in the Lord when others may try to lead you away from his guidance and love.

My soul clings to the dust; revive me according to your word.

PSALM 119:25

When you are at your lowest point, when nothing seems like it can be right, pray to God. He will raise you up and revive your spirit.

I cried to the Lord in my distress, and he responded to me.

PSALM 120:1

It may seem difficult to keep faith when things aren't going according to plan, but God speaks through others. Look for His words in good people when the next step is unclear.

No one can serve two masters, because either he will hate one and love the other, or be loyal to one and despise the other. You cannot serve God and riches!

MATTHEW 6:24

Your priorities define your life. Pursue things that feed your soul and make you virtuous rather than distracting, ego-boosting things like money and power.

Jesus told him: 'You must love the Lord your God with all your heart, with all your soul, and with all your mind.' This is the greatest and most important commandment. The second is exactly like it: 'You must love your neighbor as yourself.'

MATTHEW 22:37-39

You must know God's love before you can give love to others. Once you know his Word, you will know what is right to do in life.

Therefore, humble yourselves under the mighty hand of God, so that at the proper time he may exalt you. Throw all your worry on him, because he cares for you. Be clear-minded and alert. Your opponent, the Devil, is prowling around like a roaring lion, looking for someone to devour.

PETER 5:6-8

Look for the little things that lead you to do wrong every day and find ways to ignore them with prayer. Even if it leads you to say one more kind word, you've taken a step in the right direction.

Keep your lives free from the love of money, and be content with what you have, for God has said, "I will never leave you or abandon you." Hence we can confidently say, "The Lord is my helper; I will not be afraid. What can anyone do to me?"

HEBREWS 13:5-6

Material things and money will not buffer you from hardship. Strength, drawn from your loved ones and Christ, will be your foundation to endure anything.

On days when I am afraid, I put my trust in you.

PSALM 56:3

Fear is a normal reaction to unknown and daunting situations. Know you can rely on the Lord in those times, and embrace the wisdom that will come from Him.

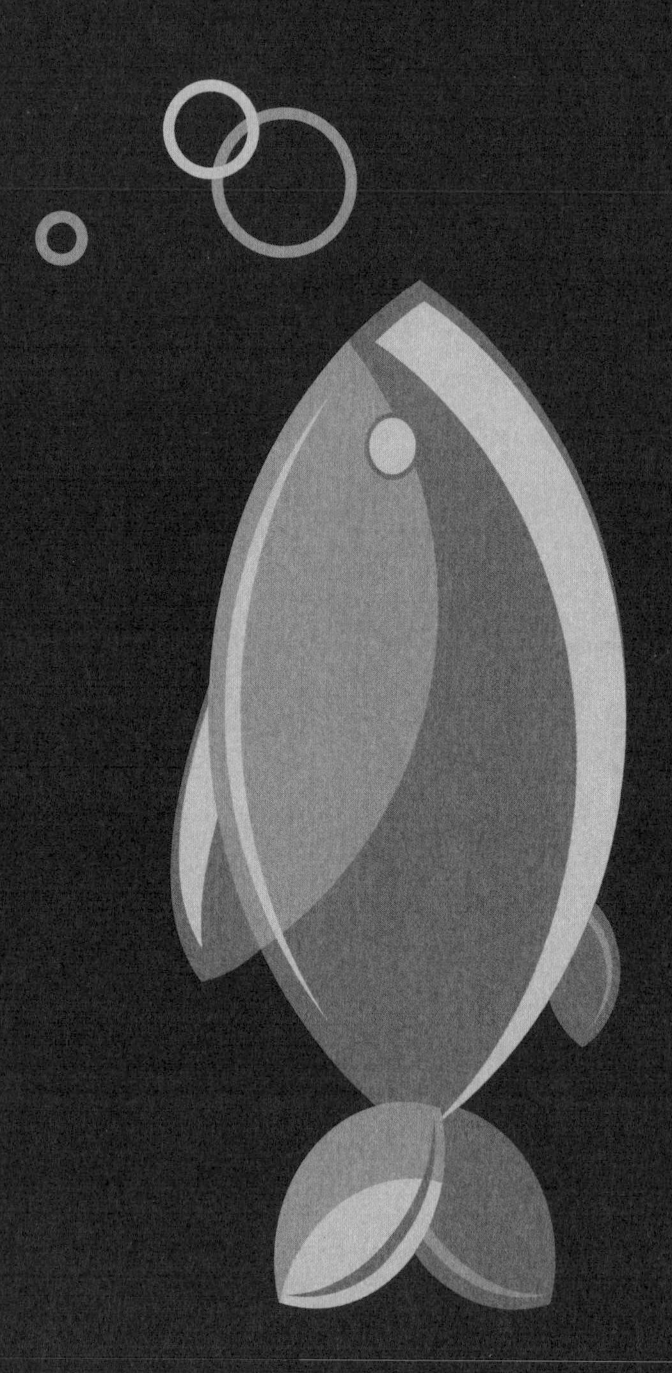

LOVE

And you must love the Lord your God with all your heart, with all your soul, with all your mind, and with all your strength.

MARK 12:30

Loving God and others requires more than simply a word or a thought. Real love requires constant attention and sacrifice, with all your actions aiming toward that goal.

Whatever you want people to do for you, do the same for them.

LUKE 6:31

Though people may seem like strangers, most want the same things in life as you do. Be kind and charitable with everyone, as you wish the same from others.

No one shows greater love than when he lays down his life for his friends.

JOHN 15:13

While most of us will not have to prove our friendship with death, a true friend will sacrifice in other ways. Letting go of selfishness is a great mark of love.

Your love must be without hypocrisy. Abhor what is evil; cling to what is good.

ROMANS 12:9

Waste little time dwelling on negative situations and emotions. To truly love others and love life, your mind must always be focused on your purpose.

A man with many friends can still be ruined, but a true friend sticks closer than a brother.

PROVERBS 18:24

It takes time and wisdom to truly realize what people are good to have in your life. A sign of a true friend is their willingness to sacrifice for you.

Dear friends, let us continuously love one another, because love comes from God. Everyone who loves has been born from God and knows God.

1 JOHN 4:7

Everyone has the Lord within them and the ability to do great works. Try to see that potential in everyone, however lost they may be.

There is no fear where love exists. Rather, perfect love banishes fear, for fear involves punishment, and the person who lives in fear has not been perfected in love. We love because God first loved us.

1 JOHN 4:18-19

Fear in relationships comes partly from doubt and self-preservation. Real love compels us to abandon these thoughts and accept the possibility of pain.

Instead, love your enemies, do good to them, and lend to them, expecting nothing in return. Then your reward will be great, and you will be children of the Most High, because He is kind even to ungrateful and evil people.

LUKE 6:35

Be generous even when you are inclined not to be. A kind gesture to an unkind person can sometimes wake up their conscience.

Husbands, love your wives as the Messiah loved the church and gave himself for it.

EPHESIANS 5:25

Marriage can only be enriching if a couple is willing to constantly work on the love and care that it demands.

Above all, clothe yourselves with love, which ties everything together in unity.

COLOSSIANS 3:14

Love is not gifts and material attributes, but a desire to cherish other people, even strangers. If that is your focus, all other good qualities will follow.

Love is patient, love is kind. It does not envy, it does not boast, it is not proud. It does not dishonor others, it is not self-seeking, it is not easily angered, it keeps no record of wrongs. Love does not delight in evil but rejoices with the truth. It always protects, always trusts, always hopes, always perseveres. Love never fails.

1 CORINTHIANS 13:4-8

To truly love requires self-awareness. Know what makes you pick silly fights or avoid generosity and try to improve your character over time.

But the fruit of the Spirit is love, joy, peace, patience, kindness, goodness, faithfulness, gentleness, and self-control. There is no law against such things.

GALATIANS 5:22-23

Being kind can make you feel vulnerable, but practice doing so anyway. You'll create more happiness in your life than if you avoided kindness.

A person's anxiety weighs down his heart, but an appropriate word is encouraging.

PROVERBS 12:25

Do not add to your own worries or the worries of others. Offer kindness and perspective to your friends for every struggle.

The Lord your God among you is powerful—he will save and he will take joyful delight in you. In his love he will renew you with his love; he will celebrate with singing because of you.

ZEPHANIAH 3:17

God is always watching and caring for your successes and failures. Know that you always have a champion in Him.

I, therefore, the prisoner of the Lord, urge you to live in a way that is worthy of the calling to which you have been called, demonstrating all expressions of humility, gentleness, and patience, accepting one another in love.

EPHESIANS 4:1-2

Though we often praise boldness and competition, it should not be the primary way we choose to relate to other people.

For I am convinced that neither death, nor life, nor angels, nor rulers, nor things present, nor things to come, nor powers, nor anything above, nor anything below, nor anything else in all creation can separate us from the love of God that is ours in union with the Messiah Jesus, our Lord.

ROMANS 8:38-39

Nothing except your own mind can separate you from Christ. Though others can influence your thinking, no one can take your faith from you.

Right now three things remain: faith, hope, and love. But the greatest of these is love.

1 CORINTHIANS 13:13

When it seems difficult to believe in Christ or to hope in the future, rely on love to see you through. Accept the love of your friends and family in times of doubt.

You will keep perfectly peaceful the one whose mind remains focused on you, because He remains in you.

ISAIAH 26:3

Know that God has placed certain challenges before you because he believes you can take them on with grace and goodness.

Above all, continue to love each other deeply, because love covers a multitude of sins.

1 PETER 4:8

Love brings out the best decisions when dealing with others. It allows us to forgive when we have been wronged, and be charitable when someone is in need.

A friend loves at all times, and a brother is there for times of trouble.

PROVERBS 17:17

No one needs to be happy all the time. The people who truly love you will stand by you and comfort you in your time of need.

This is how we have come to know love: the Messiah gave his life for us. We, too, ought to give our lives for our brothers. Whoever has earthly possessions and notices a brother in need and yet withholds his compassion from him, how can the love of God be present in him? Little children, we must stop expressing love merely by our words and manner of speech; we must love also in action and in truth.

1 JOHN 3:16-18

Praising God is simply one aspect of loving Him fully. The true test comes in how we choose to treat others, even in tiny, daily decisions.

The person who does not love does not know God, because God is love.

1 JOHN 4:8

Your relationship to God will have a ripple effect on every part of your life. It can make you more conscientious of others' needs and your life's purpose.

Love never does anything that is harmful to its neighbor. Therefore, love is the fulfillment of the Law.

ROMANS 13:10

Love should always be your guiding light in how you treat others. God will never fault a sincere good act toward your fellow man.

STRENGTH

Don't be afraid, because I'm with you; don't be anxious, because I am your God. I keep on strengthening you; I'm truly helping you. I'm surely upholding you with my victorious right hand.

ISAIAH 41:10

A setback is not the end of a journey. God is always waiting for you to invite him to aid your struggle.

But as for you, Lord, do not be far away from me;
My Strength, come quickly to help me.

PSALM 22:19

It may often feel that God is nowhere to be found, but have patience. He is always beside you, helping you endure hardship.

I pray that he would give you, according to his glorious riches, strength in your inner being and power through his Spirit.

EPHESIANS 3:16

The Holy Spirit can act through us, if we are receptive to God's message. There is endless love and strength to be drawn from it.

He said: "I love you, Lord, my strength."

PSALM 18:1

We all feel helpless and vulnerable at times. Never be ashamed to love God and admit you need His help to carry on.

I can do all things through him who strengthens me.

PHILIPPIANS 4:13

If you have a dream that you're afraid to pursue, pray to the Lord. Call on him for strength to start your journey.

Consider it pure joy, my brothers, when you are involved in various trials, because you know that the testing of your faith produces endurance. But you must let endurance have its full effect, so that you may be mature and complete, lacking nothing.

JAMES 1:2-4

Everything in life requires hard work. The ability to endure struggle is the mark of a person who is willing to experience the world fully and reap its gifts.

He's the one who gives might to the faint,
renewing strength for the powerless.

ISAIAH 40:29

The Scriptures stress the need to help the poor. Serve those who are in need of help, and God will do the same in your darkest times.

"Lord, be gracious to us; we long for you; and be our strength every morning, our salvation in times of trouble."

ISAIAH 33:2

Little everyday stresses can take a toll on your mental well-being. When you're feeling overwhelmed, say a quick prayer and hand your burdens to God.

I have set the Lord before me continuously; because he stands at my right hand, I will stand firm.

PSALM 16:8

You are never beyond God's reach. Even in the worst situation, on the worst day, you can still turn to Him.

I weep because of sorrow;
fortify me according to your word.

PSALM 119:28

Sadness can be an emotion that consumes all others. When it feels as though there is nothing that can cheer you up, lay your troubles before God. Be open to the solution He provides, even if it's contrary to your ideas.

Come to me, all of you who are weary and loaded down with burdens, and I will give you rest. Place my yoke on you and learn from me, because I am gentle and humble, and you will find rest for your souls, because my yoke is pleasant, and my burden is light.

MATTHEW 11:28-30

Like Christ, be a rock when others need your shoulder to lean on. A good friend will return the favor in due time.

For God did not give us a spirit of timidity but one of power, love, and self-discipline.

2 TIMOTHY 1:7

God did not make man to live in fear of the world, but to explore it, love it, and care for it.

Remain alert. Keep standing firm in your faith. Keep on being courageous and strong.

1 CORINTHIANS 16:13

Be thankful and appreciate the good things in your life when the bad ones start to pile up.

Be strong and courageous. Don't fear or tremble before them, because the Lord your God will be the one who keeps on walking with you—He won't leave you or abandon you.

DEUTERONOMY 31:6

Ask God to not let your small problems become bigger than necessary. Keeping them in perspective will make life easier and happier.

Those who keep waiting for the Lord will renew their strength. Then they'll soar on wings like eagles; they'll run and not grow weary; they'll walk and not grow tired.

ISAIAH 40:31

Rely on God to help you get back up after being knocked down, and both your character and your faith will grow.

The name of the Lord is a strong tower;
a righteous person rushes to it and is
lifted up above the danger.

PROVERBS 18:10

Remember that all suffering is temporary. Life is a fluid, roaming river—you are never stuck in one place.

Don't be afraid, because I'm with you; don't be anxious, because I am your God. I keep on strengthening you; I'm truly helping you. I'm surely upholding you with my victorious right hand.

ISAIAH 41:10

It is okay to feel weak and hopeless in the face of an overwhelming struggle. With prayer, try to understand the source of these feelings rather than succumbing to them.

God is our refuge and strength, a great help in times of distress. Therefore we will not be frightened when the earth roars, when the mountains shake in the depths of the seas, when its waters roar and rage, when the mountains tremble despite their pride.

PSALM 46:1-3

Though the world may seem chaotic and unfair, Christ waits in the darkness and will lead you through any trial. Pray to Christ, because He has survived true suffering.

This is what comforts me in my troubles:
that what you say revives me.

PSALM 119:50

You only get one chance to live your life. Be thankful to God for the ability to feel joy, love, comfort, and even pain.

Finally, be strong in the Lord, relying on his mighty strength.

EPHESIANS 6:10

Use God's guidance to become the best version of yourself possible. With your virtues set in stone , you can withstand anything.

PEACE

He also told them, "Go eat the best food, drink the best wine, and give something to those who have nothing, since this day is holy to our Lord. Don't be sorrowful, because the joy of the Lord is your strength."

NEHEMIAH 8:10

Create good will by sharing your fortune with your neighbors. When people feel that they are cared for, a peaceful community is built.

Let the peace of the Messiah also rule in your hearts, to which you were called in one body, and be thankful.

COLOSSIANS 3:15

When faced with conflict, avoid the urge to win the fight. Always be willing to compromise or come to an understanding.

Now may the Lord of peace give you his peace at all times and in every way. May the Lord be with all of you.

2 THESSALONIANS 3:16

Though others may create strife and pain in your life, wish only peace in their lives. You will find inner harmony by following Christ's example.

Two are better than one, because they have a good return for their labor. If they stumble, the first will lift up his friend—but woe to anyone who is alone when he falls and there is no one to help him get up.

ECCLESIASTES 4:9-10

Ego can keep you from accepting help when it is necessary for success.

I'm leaving you at peace. I'm giving you my own peace. I'm not giving it to you as the world gives. So don't let your hearts be troubled, and don't be afraid.

JOHN 14:27

Peace is hard to come by because people fail to see themselves in others. Though someone may look strange or foreign to you, judge them as you would yourself.

That's why we are not discouraged. No, even if outwardly we are wearing out, inwardly we are being renewed each and every day. This light, temporary nature of our suffering is producing for us an everlasting weight of glory, far beyond any comparison, because we do not look for things that can be seen but for things that cannot be seen. For things that can be seen are temporary, but things that cannot be seen are eternal.

2 CORINTHIANS 4:16-18

Dwelling on death may create unnecessary fear and a focus on the material. In the end, peace comes from knowing that your love and generosity will live on in others' lives.

They love to have the places of honor at festivals, the best seats in the synagogues, to be greeted in the marketplaces, and to be called 'Rabbi' by people. "But you are not to be called 'Rabbi,' because you have only one teacher, and all of you are brothers.

MATTHEW 23:6-8

People who value status over developing their inner virtue will not find satisfaction, and will always chase more accolades.

For this is how God loved the world: He gave his uniquely existing Son so that everyone who believes in him would not be lost but have eternal life.

JOHN 3:16

God loves the world, but also each of us individually. We are all special in God's eyes, and he made the ultimate sacrifice of His son for us.

Let us fix our attention on Jesus, the pioneer and perfector of the faith, who, in view of the joy set before him, endured the cross, disregarding its shame, and has sat down at the right hand of the throne of God.

HEBREWS 12:2

Christ, as the ultimate example of faith, followed God's plan though it required Him to give Himself for others.

The thief comes only to steal, slaughter, and destroy. I've come that they may have life, and have it abundantly.

JOHN 10:10

The world does not only exist to give resources. It requires us to give back with love and stewardship to people and the earth.

Therefore, make it your habit to confess your sins to one another and to pray for one another, so that you may be healed. The prayer of a righteous person is powerful and effective.

JAMES 5:16

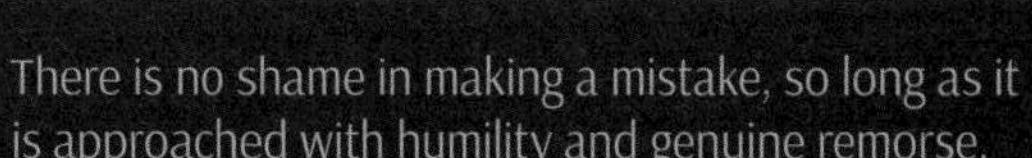
There is no shame in making a mistake, so long as it is approached with humility and genuine remorse.

I have told you this so that through me you may have peace. In the world you'll have trouble, but be courageous—I've overcome the world!

JOHN 16:33

Christ overcame the most painful, torturous trial that any human could undergo. Follow His example when facing a task that seems impossible, especially when it will help others.

Observe the blameless! Take note of the upright!
Indeed, the future of that man is peace.

PSALM 37:37

Follow those who do good and have wisdom to offer you. Remember that the best people are not always the most rich, beautiful, or powerful.

"For the mountains may collapse and the hills may reel, but my gracious love will not depart from you, neither will my covenant of peace totter," says the Lord, who has compassion on you.

ISAIAH 54:10

Aim to be like God, whose love can withstand every trial and is willingly given to all.

Then Joseph sent his brothers away, and they left for home. As they were leaving, Joseph admonished them, "Don't quarrel on the way back!"

GENESIS 45:24

You will have many companions in your life's journey. Appreciate their differences and always look for ways to improve each other's lives.

I'll give peace in the land so that you'll lie down without fear. I'll remove wildbeasts from the land, and not even war will come to your land.

LEVITICUS 26:6

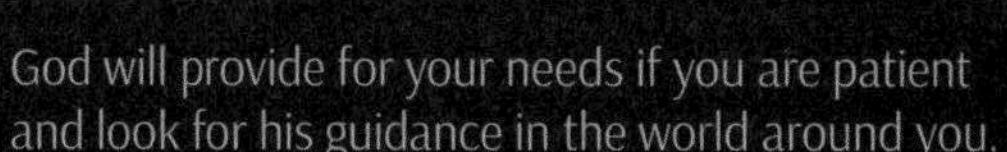
God will provide for your needs if you are patient and look for his guidance in the world around you.

Avoid evil and do good! Seek peace and pursue it!

PSALM 34:14

While the rules of living a Christian life seem simple, they are immensely difficult to follow. It may be tempting to fall into cynicism, but the best response to failure is to try again.

Anyone who overlooks an offense promotes love, but someone who gossips separates close friends.

PROVERBS 17:9

Learn to forgive and move on when a friend has wronged you. If they have sincerely apologized, don't open up old wounds by mentioning their fault.

Because if you forgive people their offenses,
your heavenly Father will also forgive you.

MATTHEW 6:14

Follow the example of the Lord and let go of grudges. Be charitable with your love though your pride and anger will tempt you to resist.

The friend shows gracious love for his friend, even if he has forsaken the fear of the Almighty.

JOB 6:14

Those who forget to love their fellow man have distanced themselves from God.

His mouth is as smooth as butter, while war is in his heart. His words were as smooth as olive oil, while his sword is drawn.

PSALM 55:21

Some people will not have your best interests at heart. Be wary of them, but offer kindness to counter their ill will.

I will lie down and sleep in peace, for you alone,
Lord, enable me to live securely.

PSALM 4:8

Approach life and its little annoyances with calm. Your attitude will spread to everyone around you, and you will inspire those who are anxious and afraid.

But he delights in the Lord's instruction, and
meditates in his instruction day and night.

PSALM 1:2

Pray and study God's Word and you will find peace in knowing the struggles of those who came before you.

KNOWLEDGE

It was for my good that I was humbled;
so that I would learn your statutes.

PSALM 119:71

Wisdom comes from experience, and some experiences are a trial that will lead to growth.

What, then, can we say about all of this? If God is for us, who can be against us?

ROMANS 8:31

Fear nothing. Know that with God at your side, not even death can claim you in eternity.

For in the gospel God's righteousness is being revealed from faith to faith, as it is written, "The righteous will live by faith."

ROMANS 1:17

Reflection: Though you may never see or touch God in life, search for him in those you love and in the world around you.

Don't make friends with a hot-tempered man, and do not associate with someone who is easily angered, or you may learn his ways and find yourself caught in a trap.

PROVERBS 22:24-25

People who are angry create anger in others. Know when to separate yourself from people who seek discord, and respond to their tantrums with a calm demeanor.

An open rebuke is better than unspoken love.
Wounds from someone who loves are trustworthy,
but kisses from an enemy speak volumes.

PROVERBS 27:5-6

The truth can be an unpleasant thing, so don't reject it if it comes from someone you trust. Knowing you faults can help you improve them.

Whoever keeps company with the wise becomes wise,
but the companion of fools suffers harm.

PROVERBS 13:20

Just as your habits affect others, those of your friends will affect you. While no one is perfect, aim to be around people who are striving to be better human beings.

You adulterers! Don't you know that friendship with the world means hostility with God? So whoever wants to be a friend of this world is an enemy of God.

JAMES 4:4

Life will provide many distractions from what is important. Turn to prayer when it is difficult to sort out your priorities.

Train a child in the way appropriate for him, and when he becomes older, he will not turn from it.

PROVERBS 22:6

Though children may rebel, they take good lessons with them. Be patient and not demanding, as Christ is with his followers.

Therefore, if anyone is in the Messiah, he is a new creation. Old things have disappeared, and—look!—all things have become new!

2 CORINTHIANS 5:17

God will always be beside you in every stage of your life, with every change that you undergo as a person.

The Lord your God will raise up for you a prophet like me from among you, from your fellow Israelites. You must listen to him.

DEUTERONOMY 18:15 NIV

Staying set in your ways keeps your mind and soul from growing. Listen to people who have different ideas from you, especially if they reflect God's will.

Grab hold of my instruction in lieu of money and knowledge instead of the finest gold

PROVERBS 8:10

Aim to grow your mind and soul, rather than your wealth. Wisdom and love last longer than trinkets.

The fear of the Lord is the beginning of knowledge, but fools despise wisdom and discipline.

PROVERBS 1:7

Even if something is contrary to your opinions, learn about it anyway. Foolish people close themselves off from new ideas and new opportunities to be virtuous.

O give your servant an understanding mind to govern your people, so I can discern between good and evil. Otherwise, how will I be able to govern this great people of yours?

1 KINGS 3:9

When faced with a big responsibility, turn to God for guidance on how to use authority to better others and treat them well.

Now, go! I myself will help you with your speech,
and I'll teach you what you are to say.

EXODUS 4:12

Sometimes it is difficult to know the right thing to say. Pray to the Lord and meditate to find the words within yourself.

You have been shown this in order to know that 'the Lord is God' and there is no one like Him.

DEUTERONOMY 4:35

It is tempting to replace God with other idols and preoccupations, but only your faith will provide the right path forward in life.

"Lord, why can't I follow you now?" Peter asked him. "I would lay down my life for you!"

JOHN 13:37

Sometimes the most dramatic act isn't the right one. Trust in God to guide you to what is right, which sometimes is merely showing restraint in anger or distress.

This is the day that the Lord has made;
let's rejoice and be glad in it.

PSALM 118:24

Take joy in the wonders of the world, in love and nature, and don't be distracted by its petty demands.

Therefore, as you go, disciple people in all nations, baptizing them in the name of the Father, and the Son, and the Holy Spirit.

MATTHEW 28:19

Lead others to the Lord by example. Words may turn people away, but your actions are irrefutable proof of His love and guidance.

So I say to you: Keep asking, and it will be given you. Keep searching, and you will find. Keep knocking, and the door will be opened for you.

LUKE 11:9

Search always, be curious, and don't be afraid to explore new things. The Lord will always provide for you in your journey.

CREDITS

N K/Shutterstock
Ekaterina Brusnika/Shutterstock
Mike Tan/Shutterstock
otsphoto/Shutterstock
Barna Tanko/Shutterstock
Linn Currie/Shutterstock
Olga_i/Shutterstock
Joop Snijder Photography/
Shutterstock
DragoNika/Shutterstock
Gerard Koudenburg/Shutterstock
Vitaly Titov & Maria Sidelnikova/
Shutterstock
ashin Georgiy/Shutterstock
Zuzule/Shutterstock
gorillaimages/Shutterstock
Mat Hayward/Shutterstock
Tatiana Katsai/Shutterstock
S Curtis/Shutterstock
AnetaPics/Shutterstock
Savo Ilic/Shutterstock
ZIGROUP-CREATIONS/Shutterstock
Rita Kochmarjova/Shutterstock
dezi/Shutterstock
Ollyy/Shutterstock
Anna Tyurina/Shutterstock
oloviova Liudmyla/Shutterstock
PHOTOCREO Michal Bednarek/
Shutterstock
Zbigniew Guzowski/Shutterstock
gurinaleksandr/Shutterstock
Ksenia Merenkova/Shutterstock
Evgeny Bakharev/Shutterstock
Brian Guest/Shutterstock
Makarova Viktoria/Shutterstock
Jaromir Chalabala/Shutterstock
MichaelHansen/Shutterstock
AlexussK/Shutterstock
rebeccaashworth/Shutterstock
Sergei Bashkatov/Shutterstock
Alan Mardi/Shutterstock
photomim/Shutterstock
Utekhina Anna/Shutterstock
leungchopan/Shutterstock
Denisa Doudova/Shutterstock
Vera Zinkova/Shutterstock
Nikol Mansfeld/Shutterstock
Nataliya_Ostapenko/Shutterstock
Ksenia Raykova/Shutterstock
Liliya Kulianionak/Shutterstock
cynoclub/Shutterstock
Eduard Kyslynskyy/Shutterstock
Nikolai Tsvetkov/Shutterstock
Mikkel Bigandt/Shutterstock
Fribus Mara/Shutterstock
tsik/Shutterstock
Hysteria/Shutterstock
Francesco Dazzi/Shutterstock
AleksandrN/Shutterstock
Little Moon/Shutterstock
V.Borisov/Shutterstock
Lenkadan/Shutterstock
atyana Vyc/Shutterstock
Ammit Jack/Shutterstock
Patryk Kosmider/Shutterstock
dexter_cz/Shutterstock
Dora Zett/Shutterstock
Iryna Dobrovynska/Shutterstock
Lukas Rebec/Shutterstock
Sari ONeal/Shutterstock
sergioboccardo/Shutterstock
sunsinger/Shutterstock
Yurkovska Tanya/Shutterstock
Sheeva1/Shutterstock
Ilya Frankazoid/Shutterstock
Volodymyr Burdiak/Shutterstock
TDway/Shutterstock
KellyNelson/Shutterstock
Sergey Chirkov/Shutterstock
Fotyma

Mango Publishing, established in 2014, publishes an eclectic list of books by diverse authors—both new and established voices—on topics ranging from business, personal growth, women's empowerment, LGBTQ studies, health, and spirituality to history, popular culture, time management, decluttering, lifestyle, mental wellness, aging, and sustainable living. We were recently named 2019's #1 fastest growing independent publisher by *Publishers Weekly*. Our success is driven by our main goal, which is to publish high quality books that will entertain readers as well as make a positive difference in their lives.

Our readers are our most important resource; we value your input, suggestions, and ideas. We'd love to hear from you—after all, we are publishing books for you!

Please stay in touch with us and follow us at:

Facebook: Mango Publishing
Twitter: @MangoPublishing
Instagram: @MangoPublishing
LinkedIn: Mango Publishing
Pinterest: Mango Publishing

Sign up for our newsletter at www.mango.bz and receive a free book!

Join us on Mango's journey to reinvent publishing, one book at a time.